Seditious Preachers, Ungodly Teachers

"Inter Folia Fructus."

SEDITIOUS

Preachers,

UNGODLY

TEACHERS.

"History is but the Unrolled Scroll of Prophecy."
—James A. Garfield.

PRIVATELY PRINTED
FOR THE CLARENDON HISTORICAL SOCIETY.

1887.

SEDITIOUS

PREACHERS,

UNGODLY

TEACHERS.

EXEMPLIFIED,

In the Cafe of the Minifters, Ejected by the Act of Uniformity 1662, who appear to have been the only **Trumpets** to **War**, and **Incendiaries** towards **Rebellion**, from their own Printed Sermons, and My Lord *Clarendon's* Hiftory.

Oppofed chiefly to Mr. *Callamy's Abridgment*, where he has Canonized them for fo many *Saints* and *Confeffors*, to the great Encouragement of all Thofe, who fhall ever after Act by, and Avow the like Rebellious Principles and Practices.

Ex Ore tuo.

If the Perfon, and the Place, can improve and aggravate the Offence (as without doubt it doth, both before God and Man) methinks the Preaching Treafon and Rebellion out of the Pulpits, fhould be worfe than the advancing it in the Market, as much as poyfoning a Man at the Communion would be worfe than Murthering him at a Tavern. *Clarendon's* Hift. of Rebell. Vol. 2. p. 19.

The *Independents* and *Prefbyterians* were equally Mafters of Diffimulation, and had equally Malice and Wickednefs in their Intentions, tho' not of the fame kind, and were equally unreftrained by any Scruples, or Motions, of Confcience. *Ibid.* Vol. 3. p. 82.

London, Printed, and Sold for *J. Morphew* near *Stationer's-Hall.* 1709.

THE PREFACE.

IT'S possible these Sheets may fall into some Hands, who in this Moderate Age, may think it too invidious a Subject to look back, and reflect, on the many Villanies, and bloody Treasons, carried on, and accomplished by the Faction in the Last Age. One year of which afforded so much Matter for our Horror and Amazement; "That a Noble Historian thinks the Memory of all its Transactions ought to be rais'd out of all Records, least by the success of it, Atheism, Infidelity, and Rebellion should be propagated in the World." The Writer therefore of this Piece thinks it necessary to declare the Reasons, which induced him to the Publication of it; least he might be thought to take delight in perpetuating Heats and Animosities, and in keeping up odious Names and Distinctions.

If the pernicious Principles of the Incendiaries of those times, had been buried with them in their Graves; or had they left the least Memorial of their Penitence behind them, then indeed Christian Charity, and Candor, would have commanded a Silence and Oblivion amongst Men : But when they shall Brave it out to their Dying Hours, and their Lives shall afterwards be deliver'd down to Posterity, as fit Examples for their Imitation and Instruction. Then whoever undertakes to lay open their Crimes, and expose their Hypocrisies, with a design to stop and prevent the ill Influence, their contagious Examples might have upon this Age too much inclined to call Evil Good, that Man transgresseth not the Bounds of Charity and

5

Moderation, nor offendeth against any Duties either sacred or humane.

The Writer therefore of this Pamphlet was moved with an honest Zeal and just Indignation, to find a Bold Sectarian Preacher undertake to Canonize for Saints, and Confessors, those very Men, whom the best Historians had branded with lasting marks of Infamy;[*] and whilst their Printed Sermons still remained upon Record, as so many Monuments of their Guilt in sounding the Trumpet to War, against their Most Gracious Sovereign. Methinks it was a strange Introduction of this Age to begin it with Printed Harangues in Commemoration of those Men, whose misguided Zeal had filled the former Age with Blood and Confusion, and it was as odd a way of ushering in the Reign of our Most Glorious Queen so publickly to vindicate the Memories of those Men, who had so barbarously treated her Royal Grandfather K. Charles I. For what sincere obedience, and respect, can Her Majesty expect from those Men, who think their Names deserve to be Embalmed, who did actually represent the best of Princes, as more a Nero, than Nero himself, who pursued him with their venemous Tongues from Palace to Palace, from Camp to Camp, from Prison to Prison ; nay, at length, to the Scaffold itself ; and afterwards wrote in Defence of his Murder, calling it an Honourable Sentence, that might be justified from clear Texts of Scripture, and from the Pulpit declared his Destruction to be just and righteous ; of all which particular Accusations, some one or other of the most Dignified Saints in Calamy's Calendar were most highly guilty of.

And must not this Race of Men be for ever Factious and Seditious, if Those who rise up in their Rooms, do but imitate their Examples, and partake of the same Spirit, whereby they were acted, which is so much desired and recommended by Mr. Calamy ; Now if he would be understood only to respect the latter part of these Men's Lives, when they were silenced and ejected; it ought likewise to be considered, that no one of these Incendiaries, howsoever guilty, did ever show the least remorse of Conscience, or Penitence, for their

[*] Calamy's Abridgment.

former seditious Practices, but on the contrary, continued to Libel and Defame both Church and State, even after they had received extraordinary Marks of Mercy and Forgiveness ; and for any one to talk of such Mens being acted with a Divine Spirit, of being guided and assisted with the Prefence of God, is making very bold with that sacred tremendous Name, and is a high Profanation of Religion, and favours much of the formal Cant and Hypocrisy of the Times.

I may venture to move my Reader with Mr. Calamy to view his List of Confessors, and desire him to observe what manner of Men they were, who were the Spoils and Triumphs of Uniformity, and he will there find the very small number of Learn'd and Worthy Men so obscured, and hid, in a Crowd of wild Enthsiuasts and ignorant Mechanicks, that he must view and review them, before he can discover them. · Besides, an Impartial Observer will look back and consider, by what Methods, and by whose Patronage these Men filled the Church, and from thence be able to form a right Judgment of the Qualifications and Abilities of the Ministers, who were ejected by the Act of Uniformity. Is any thing more evident ! than that Those who had the ascendency of Affairs through the whole Kingdom, made it their Business for many Years to bring an Illiterate Ministry into the Church ; and that the surest way to Preferment, was, the most ready compliance to their Usurpation ; now that such Tools and Little Creatures of State should become Men of such Publick Ministerial Abilities and Usefulness,* as no Age or Country have produced the like, seems a thing incredible, whether we have respect to their Educations, their Printed Discourses, or to the deplorable State of Religion, which in their Times, was nothing but Cant and Enthusiasm.

Let us take a view of the Priests and Religion of those Times from the Mouth of one of their own most noted Writers, who thus expostulates with their Reforming Parliament ;† " You have done,.

---

* See Hist. of England Vol. 3. p. 192.
† Preface to Edward's Gangræna.

says he, worthily against Prelates, scandalous Ministers and
Ceremonies, but what have you done against other kinds of growing
Evils, Heresies, Schisms, and Disorders : You have made a
Reformation, but with it have we not a Deformation, and worse
things come in upon us than ever we had before ? You have put
down the Common Prayer, and there are Many amongst us have put
down the Scriptures, you have cast out Ceremonies in the Sacraments,
and we have many cast out the Sacraments themselves, you have put
down Saints Days, and we have Many make nothing at all of the
Lord's Day ; in the Bishops Days, we had the Fourth Commandment
taken away, but now we have all the Ten ; the worst of Prelates had
many sound Doctrines, and had many commendable Practices, but
Many Sects in our Day deny all Principles of Religion, are Enemies
to all holy Duties, Order, and Learning ; in the Bishop's Days, we
had many unlearned Ministers, and have we not now a Company of
Jeroboam's Priests ? You have destroyed Baal and his Priests, but
have you been zealous against Golden Calves, and the Priests of the
Lowest of the people ?"   This account of the Presbyterian Reformation was wrote within Four Years after the Extirpation of Episcopacy ;
judge ye therefore to what an amazing height, Ignorance, Profaneness,
Atheism, and Rebellion must necessarily grow in so fruitful a Soil,
after many Years longer Continuance to encrease and multiply in.
From hence we may learn, what various Disorders and endless
Confusions we must expect, if ever the Adherers to the Puritanical
Principle, of the necessity of a further Reformation in the Church,
should have their Liberties to reform Religion to their Humours : Is
it not highly probable, they would sit like their Westminster Assembly
so long in finding out a New Religion, that at last they would leave
none at all ?

But let us return to Calamy's Confessors, whom we are told were
of the Lowest of the People, and like to Jeroboam's Priests ; its well,
he was not of the Laudensian Faction, who gave this Character of
them, for then it would have been thought horridly Censorious,
and an insufferable Injury ; how often is poor Antony a Wood the

Subject of Calamy's Scorn and Reproach, because he did not think so favourably of them, as Calamy does ; Mr. Wood indeed gave his Characters with great Truth and Impartiality, neither denying them their due Praises, nor industriously concealing their Faults ; which is the Business of a Faithful Historian, whereas Mr. Calamy, though he gives the particular Characters of several Hundred Persons, yet throws all their Faults behind the Curtain, and wont allow of any Blemish, or Miscarriage, in any one Instance ; and what makes him to be more inexcusable, is, that he only pretends to be the Abridger of Baxter's Life, who with great Freedom laid open their Faults, when he had mentioned their supposed Virtues ; nay, I can instance in one memorable Name, whom Mr. B. represents as a meer State Jugler, as one who was the greatest Encourager and main Stickler in all the various Changes of the Times, and the greatest Opposer of Peace and Concord ; what can be more sharp or biting, than these Reflections of Mr. Baxter's upon some of Dr. Owen's seditious Practices?* Oh! What may not Pride doe? And what Miscarriages will not false Principles and Faction hide? And taking Occasion to mention his Writings, The Doctor, says he, being neither able to repent (hitherto) or to justify himself, must be silent, or only plead the Act of Oblivion. In short, he thought the Doctor gave great Advantage to their Adversaries for Reproach, and that he occasioned a general Injury to the Nonconformists. Whereas Mr. B. faithful Abridger, is full of the Doctors Praises and Virtues, and reckons him the brightest Ornament of the Age, and one of the greatest Honours to their Cause ; and then bestows some passionate Expressions on poor Antony a Wood, though he gives the Doctor a much more favourable Character than Mr. B. would allow him, the one mentioning his natural and acquired Endowments, the other having not a Word in his Favor.

There is an Instance where Mr. Calamy thought to bear hard upon Mr. Wood, but indeed betrays a strange Folly in giving so fair a

---

* See his Life Part 3. pag. 42.

Handle for an Adversary to expose him. Mr. Wood having given a
particular Account of the Sermons of a Presbyterian Preacher,* he
likewise tells us, that he preached the Funeral Sermon of J. Bradshaw
President of the High Court of Justice, that condemned King Charles
I. to Die, and that he took great Liberty in speaking much to the
Honour and Praise of that Monster of Men. Now after Mr. C. has
given as fulsom a Character of the Preacher, as he did of the
President, he then takes Mr. Wood to Task for carping at the
Preacher for this Sermon, and where is Mr. Wood's Fault? In
wondring that a Preacher of the Gospel should mount the Pulpit, and
there pronounce great Praises and Commendations on a Man, who
durst sentence his Soveraign to Death, an Action of that barbarous
amazing Nature, that the very Thoughts of it, gives a Shock to humane
Nature, and put our Spirits in a Ferment ; certainly the Preacher
ne'er designed nor thought his Auditory could entertain an ill Opinion
of Murder, Treason and Rebellion, for then they must needs have
condemn'd his deceased Hero, and wonder'd at his impious Discourse.

A late Noble Historian (with all imaginable Deference be it
mention'd) has not given a more notorious Instance of their Preachers
perverting and wresting the Scriptures to their odious Purposes than
this I am here insisting on ; for Bradshaw was hired, Judas like, for
Mony, was a Man of great Pride and Impudence, of a Bloody and
Cruel Temper beyond all Comparison, and yet the Preacher pitched
upon the following Text, as he thought most applicable to his deceased
Friend, viz. The Righteous Perisheth, and no Man layeth it to
Heart, and Merciful Men are taken away, none considering, that the
Righteous is taken away from the Evil to come. † Now if Bradshaw
was a Merciful or a Righteous Man, there never was a Cruel or
Wicked Man since the Creation, and if he was not Guilty of Crimes
against which Damnation it self is denounced, and Hell-fire prepared,
then the most Profligate Wretch, and the most daring Sinner, that
ever defied Heaven and Judgment, may hope for Mercy ; and yet it

* Mr. Rowe.   † Isaiah 57. Ch. ver. 1.

must be owned, that had the Preacher chose only the latter Part of his Text, it might have been very fitly applied to Bradshaw's Case; for had he lived but a very few Months longer, Tyburn had been his Fate, and a Halter his deserved Punishment; so that the Preacher seem'd to have spoken prophetically, when he said, that He was taken away from the Evil to come.

We are told indeed, that Julian the Apostate and Nero, had their deserved Praises, and why might not Bradshaw have his Virtues too ; It's one thing to write as an Historian, and another to speak from the Pulpit, where clapping the Title of Saint * upon a Villain and a Traytor, may very probably have a bad Influence upon the Congregation. It's very strange that Mr. Calamy can allow, that Nero had his deserved Praises, and yet wont spare one good Word in Favour of that Virtuous Prince King Charles the I. nor indeed fairly represent any one contested Action of his Life, but on the contrary, uses his utmost Art to blacken and defame his Memory, and I may safely defy him to produce any one Instance in all Mr. Baxter's voluminous Writings, where he mentions that Prince, or any of his Actions, with any tolerable respect or candor, and yet he has ventured to sanctify and defend the greatest Incendiaries, and Traytors, that any Nation was ever cursed with, and has sent them by wholesale into Heaven and everlasting Rest.

It would be endless, should I go about to enumerate all the weak and trifling Exceptions, which Mr. Calamy makes against Mr. Wood; but I can't forbear observing, how the Poor Man's Enemies are put to their Shifts and Inventions, when he is at Rest, and in his Grave, for matter, wherewith to blacken and revile him ; Mr. Calamy fancies him to have been a merry boon Companion, one that was used to pass away the tedious Hours over a Glass, diverting himself and Company with wanton Tales ; whereas an Oxonian Adversary, who doubtless knew him better, vents his Spleen against him after a very different manner, for he represents him to have been a melancholy monkish

---

* Calamy abridg. p. 208.

Scholar, confined to his Study, and a Stranger to Men and Conversation.[*]

Certainly Mr. Calamy spits his Venom against the Oxford Historiographer with a very ill Grace, when he charges him with making bitter and spiteful Reflections, which if true, only regards the Characters of a few private Persons : Whereas Mr. Calamy is very free in his Reproaches, and inveighings, against our established Laws, which the Wisdom of the Nation has provided for the Honour and Safety of our Religion, the Peace and Welfare of the Nation ; as if he had the Modesty to think that King, Lords, and Commons ought to have submitted to his Humour and Sentiments. At this Rate, the Legislative Authority may enact, what Laws they please ; but they must expect no great Regard and Reverence will be paid to them, so long as every Malapert Scribbler has the Liberty publickly to libel and censure them. "A great Man [†] once told the House of Commons, that it imported the very Essence of Parliaments to keep up the Honour of it's former Acts, and not to suffer them to be blasted from abroad ; believe me, says he, all the Reverence and Authority, which we expect from future times to our own Acts hereafter, depends upon our upholding the Dignity of what former Parliaments have done."

Methinks it's strange, that Calamy and those of his Denomination, can't be contented to be dispensed with for their Obedience to the Laws, but they must reproach, and libel them with a Malice always superior to their Understandings ; otherwise Mr. Calamy could never have represented Episcopal Government to have been most suitable to Ignorance, Carelessness, and Formality,[‡] nor have aspersed the Conforming Clergy, as Men, who minded Preferment more than real Religion :[||] In short, a Pack of meer raw, unfurnish'd Novices, and yet mark the Confidence of the Man, when he says his Abridgement hath met with Acceptance amongst Men of Temper, of all Ranks and Denominations beyond his Expectation. Whereas those very Divines,[§]

---

[*] Dr. Pope in his Life of B. Ward p. 171.
[†] Lord Digby.   [‡] p. 48.   [||] p. 491.   [§] Mr. Olliffe and Hoadly.

who have chiefly took him to Task, by refuting his Calumnies, and exposing his Malice, are Persons, who take all Opportunities to distinguish themselves for their singular Moderation to all sober Dissenters, and have jointly declared, "that they never yet knew any single Person, who did not esteem Mr. Calamy's to be an unreasonable Performance, naturally tending to revive our Differences, when the Toleration had laid this ‚matter asleep ;" and Mr. Olliffe declares, that his whole Discourse seems to him to be one continued Misrepresentation of the Terms of Conformity, by his severe and rigid Interpretations, which the Law doth not require, and when the plain Construction, and Use of Words would not only admit of, but do fairly call for another Sense without any Stretch or Force.

I cannot pass by another Instance of Calamy's great Assurance, his Prefixing the Name of a Noble Peer to his Book, which throws so much Filth and Scandal on the Royal Cause, for which the Family of that Honourable Person suffered so much, and in which they so eminently signalized themselves, and at this day so justly glory in ; whereas the Dedication carries with it this impudent Supposition, that his Lordship would disown a Cause, which has given so much Honour to his Family. My Lord Clarendon has observed upon the same Occasion, That the Modesty of this Race of People is always equal to their Obedience. And that stigmatized Wretch De Foe, the Mercenary Fool and Advocate for the Party, has given us a later Instance of the Truth and Justness of our noble Authors Observation, by presuming to dedicate to her sacred Majesty his scurrilous Ribaldry, and imploring her Royal Protection to one of the most perjured and lewdest Apostates of the Age.* But when they have a publick Party Purse to maintain and support the Cause, to be sure they will never want prostitute Pens to defend it.

The Press has swarmed with scurrilous Pamphlets against the Church, and her Bishops, ever since the Reign of Queen Elizabeth, and her Historian Camden often mentions their Billingsgate

* Abraham Gill.

Language, being fitter for Scullions in a Kitchin, than Members of a
Christian Community; and therefore must not a late Dissenting
Scribler* be nearly allied to the first born of Impudence, who in the
very Frontispiece of his Book avers, that the Dissenters Behaviour to
the Church of England was ever most Christian; and afterwards
pretends that the Rudeness at any time offered to her, proceeded from
some of the vulgar People, which ought to bring no reflection on
their Ministers; but Mr. Camden expressly says, that these Scriblers
were of the Ministry,† and more than once complains of the strange
Petulancy and sullen Haughtiness of the congregational Teachers,
inspight of all the Tenderness and prudent Forbearance of the then
Archbishop.

Was not the Authors of the Smectymnuan Libel of their Ministry,
where they call Episcopacy an Antichristian Government, from
whence Pride, Treason and Rebellion issued: Did not they revile
and asperse the very pious and moderate Bishop Hall, by calling him
an Arrogant, Confident, and Self-confounded Man, which as the
Bishop observes, are but a handful out of a full Sack; and therefore
with what Face can Mr. Palmer aver, that they never offered any
Indignities to any Sober, Pious Person of the Church's Communion:
But according to a new way of Writing, a Man may Libel and
Defame, nay, pull down and destroy the Church and Bishops, and it
must be look'd upon, as an Argument of most Christian Behavior
towards them.

Mr Palmer has likewise a pretty way with him of stating the Merits
of the Cause, by puting the Case of the Church upon the Level with
the Dissenters, as if there ought to be the same awe and restraint upon
a Man, who writes against a Pestilent Sect, or a seditious Party of
Men, as when they presume to write against our established Church
and Laws. I am sure, where ever they have Power, they restrain
People from so much as speaking against their Church Government.
They know very well, where Presbytery is so very rampant, as to

---

* Mr. Palmer.   † See Vind. p. 73.

make it High Treason, Death it self, but to speak in Defence of Episcopacy, and They now, and ever did, take what Liberty they pleased to Preach, Write, and Print against the Common Prayer-book; yet they formerly laid a severe Penalty upon Those, who wrote against their Directory.

Whoever first reads Mr. Palmer's Assertions, that the Behavior of the Dissenters to the Church was always with that Patience, Moderation, and Submission as became Christians, will be the less surprised to find him, averring,* that Their Behavior to K. Charles I. was a bright Instance of their Christian Principles, and the Reasons he offers to maintain this amazing Assertion, are equally surprising.

The first thing alleged by him is, That They never engaged but under the Conduct of the Lords and Commons of England; in answer to this, its notoriously known, that Fourscore and odd Temporal Lords espoused the Royal Cause, and attended the King's Service; and whoever considers that Number, and the Peers at that time under Age, must readily perceive how inconsiderable a Number of Peers composed the Assembly at Westminster;† for instance, there was not above Five or Six Peers present at the Passing the Ordinance for Murthering that Great Prelate Archb. Laud; and then for the House of Commons, let it be consider'd there was about Two Hundred Gentlemen of the best Estates and Quality, who attended the King at Oxford, others had retired themselves into several Counties, and yet could not through the danger of Travelling be present at Oxford; and many had withdrawn themselves into Foreign Parts, and now whoever considers the following Particulars will easily conclude, how very small the Assembly was at Westminster, and how Few had right to sit there; They themselves had voted out of the House several of their own Principal Instruments, many were at that time Imprisoned by them, many Members were factiously kept from the House from the beginning, upon questions of Elections, and many without any colour kept in, by not suffering their Elections to be

---

*P. 90.
† Rushworth's Coll. Vol. 5. p. 573.

reported, and that near Forty Members were dead, into whose Rooms no new Persons were Chosen, and many were become Barons by Descent or Creation. So that what Mr. P. calls the Lords and Commons of England, will be looked upon by an Impartial Reader, as no other than the Factious Party of them. It may perhaps be objected, that the King called them a Parliament; it's true, the King being always desirous to see the Nation restored to its former Peace and Tranquility, thought those Real Blessings were not to be hazarded by insisting upon Forms and Punctilio's.

But, then some Episcopal Lords and Commons, and Archbishop Williams in particular, engaged against the King as well as the Presbyterians.

Was the Apostles ever censured, because they had a Judas amongst them, or did that excuse the Scribes and Pharisees; and its very hard, that the Treachery of pretended Friends should be laid to the charge, and objected as a fault against the Church it self, and more unreasonable, that those should be call'd Episcopal Men, who never rested till they had extirpated Episcopacy Root and Branch, abolished the Common Prayer, and established Presbytery in its room. Does any body question under what Denomination they should place Mr. Baxter in, or does not his apostatizing from Episcopacy give the Presbyterians the pretended Honour of him, it's the Persuasion a Man lives and dyes in, not that which he was bred up in, that must determine a Man's Character: But I shall leave the farther Prosecution of this Argument to some Low Church-Man whom it chiefly concerns.

It is alledged,* that there was a high Violation of Property by the Court, and if the like should happen again a Civil War cannot be avoided.

For Arguments sake, I will grant, that the Civil Rights of the People were violated in K. Charles I. Reign; but then does it not argue an implacable hatred in the Faction to the Memory of that un-

---

* P. 44.

fortunate Prince to take all occasions to aggravate every Error and
Miscarriage of Government, and yet pass over in utter silence those
many Gracious Acts, he so readily consented to, for the taking away
all Grievances real or imaginary; Besides, the Condition of that
People must be very miserable and deservedly too, that when their
Properties have been invaded by their Prince, the most reasonable
Securities, Concessions, and Reparations shan't be thought satisfactory,
but the whole Kingdom must be set in a Flame, that their Prince may
be sure to see his Error. I think we may safely conclude, that Those
who argue after this manner, and justify the former Proceedings, are
resolved to play the Old Game over again, whenever a fitting Opportunity serves.

The whole Prosecution of Mr. Palmer's arguing upon this Head, is
one continued Series of bold Assertions; I believe he is the first
Man, who called the Late Revolution* the Second Civil War, and
compared the Proceedings of the Convention to the rebellious
Practices of the Refuse of the Two Houses in Forty One. It's first
to be observed, that if the Late Revolution was a Civil War, then
King William gained his Point by Conquest, and how the Nation
will receive such a Notion, may easily be guessed from the Fate of an
Eminent Writer; and then most of the Proceedings of that Assembly,
who took upon them the Name of the Parliament, and as such
engaged War against the King, have been reversed and annulled by
the whole Legislative Powers, with the highest Marks of Infamy and
abhorrence; nay, both Lords and Commons since the Revolution
have expressly declared their utmost dislike to the seditious Practices
of those unhappy Times: And now after all this, it's very daring for
any Private Person publickly to write in their Vindication, and
pretend to Warrant their Proceedings upon the same Grounds, and
Principles, with our Present happy Establishment; where all the
Parts of our Legal Civil Power, that could then be had, joyned in the
Exercise of that Provisional Power, which is necessary reserved to a

* P. 44.

Free People, to prevent the utter Subversion of our Constitution and the Destruction of a whole Community. But the Case of Forty One was vastly different, for then some sly and crafty Managers incensed and abused the well meaning Zealots, in order to carry on their own ambitious Designs, and at last raised their own Fortune upon the ruins of their Country, by establishing themselves in the Royal Power and Dignity, and usurping that Government into their own Hands, which by repeated Oaths they had vowed to maintain and uphold ; thus we may observe, some Men who would be thought such mighty Advocates for the Revolution, become the Rankest Libellers of it.

It's likewise alleged by Mr. Palmer,* That the King was murdered, the Republick erected, and the Usurpation supported by a little Faction, and a few of Cromwell's Partizans assisted by the Army. And so, he thinks, no ways concerns the Body of Dissenters.

Mr Palmer must entertain a very weak Opinion of his Reader, when he endeavours to perswade him into a Belief, that a Small Faction, or a Few Partizans, ever did, or can destroy the Constitution of a Government, so well cemented and established as ours was, and is known to be ; and then for the Army, it's strange if they did amiss, since we are assured, that they had so many pious, laborious, and worthy Divines to attend and instruct every Regiment : But it's plain, that the Frame of our old English Constitution was unhinged, the Authority and Power of the Laws defied, and trampled upon, before the Army was raised ; and long before the War began, may the Parliament be said to have lost its Name, and its Nature too; for when the Iniquity of the Times are so bad, as not to permit that August Assembly to sit, speak, and vote with Honour, Freedom, and Safety, when its Debates are awed, and influenced by a Tumultuary and Menacing Rabble, when things received and settled upon solemn Debates, are resumed, altered, and determined contrary to the Law and Custom of Parliaments, then is the very Being, the vital, and essential Parts of her Constitution, sunk, and destroyed, and it's notoriously

* P. 46.

evident, that this was the true State of those Times we are speaking of; and it's a manifest Absurdity to lay these Things upon the Army, because we must suppose a thing to act, before it has a Being; and then for that unhappy part, which relates to the Person of the King, it's plain, the War only accomplished and finished his Ruin, for before that begun, a prevailing Faction in the Army had despoiled him of his Royalty, and almost reduced him to the Condition of a private Person, by robbing him of his Revenue, the Militia, and other Legal Prerogatives; and I shall show hereafter, that the barbarous Murder of that King, ought not to be laid wholly to the Charge of the Army, for they acted but one Part in that deep Villany, and so ought to bear but an equal share in the Reproach of it.

Thus have I examined, and I hope refuted too, the most material Allegations brought by Mr. Palmer in Vindication of the Dissenter's Loyalty, and most Christian Behaviour to our Church, and I shall here dismiss him with these Remarks; That he has forgot to oblige the World with his Notes on my Lord Clarendon's History, which were to give more Satisfaction than the Book it self has done: Nor must he think to come off by his mysterious way of expressing himself, That his notes should come out, when the peculiar Turn that his Lordship's Principles did oblige him to give to all the Parts in his History, were removed.* Since Mr. Palmer plainly owns, that noble History does oppose, and contradict his Assertions, nor has he paid another just Debt to Mr. Westly, who was promised some mighty Matters from Mr. Palmer's severe Studies, and which was to silence Mr. Westly from any further Demands, What have you done? But notwithstanding all these vain-glorious Boastings, the Mountain has not brought forth so much as a Mouse.

It's long ago, since it was first observed, That many had repented of Presbytery, but Presbytery never had repented of any thing; and the same Charge does at this Day stand good against them. How injurious they were to King Charles I. by casting that odious Jealousie, and groundless Aspersion on him, of his designing to reduce the whole

---

* See his Preface.

Nation to Popery, by which senseless Scandal they so much distracted
the Minds of the People, and disturbed the Peace, and Settlement of
the Kingdom: And when many of these Incendiaries survived the
Passion and Fury of those Times, yet to the great Aggravation of their
Guilt, they never repented of, or made any Reparation for their
former Conduct, and not a few of them lived to see Barefaced Popery
mount the Throne, and use open Violence in carrying on her Designs;
and then these Men servilely courted, and thank her for the Breach
of those Laws, on which our Religion and Liberties depended; and
those who had been so much against Set Forms, were then content
the Priests should indite for them. What they did in that Reign,
says the present Bishop of Sarum, is well known, and cannot be
excused.* But Calamy and Palmer, tho' they affect to quote his
Lordship's Authority on many occasions, yet in this particular, they
beg his Pardon, and have endeavoured to excuse, and even to justify
their Addresses in that Reign. Mr. Baxter thought that some Romish
Priests preached to the Independent Congregations in the Times of
our Confusion, and had he not been so partial to the Presbyterians,
there was the same Reasons to believe, they shelter'd and disguised
themselves amongst that Sect, especially, when we are assured from
good Authorities, that there was a Romish Seminary at Paris, for
young Students Twice in the Week to oppose one another, one
defending Presbytery, the other Independency, and one of the
Learnedest of the Convent, took Notes, and judged of the Proficiency,
and Genius of the Disputants, and as their Fancies lay, they were to
exercise their Wits, either in Presbytery or Independency; and when
they returned to England, they were taught their Lesson to say, that
they were poor Christians, that formerly fled beyond Sea for their
Religion sake, and were returned with glad News to enjoy their
Liberty of Conscience; and we are assured,† that one Hundred of
them went over in 1646. and were most of them Soldiers in the

---

* See Letter to a Dissenter, who says, that Mony was sprinkled amongst the Dissenting Ministers. P. 9.
† See Ushers Life p. 611.

Parliament's Army. From hence, we may reasonably conclude, that a good handsome Sprinkling of them got into their pulpits, being so well qualified for the Office, and no question but in King James's Reign, they used the same Arts and Disguises. It's well known, they both used their united Strength to repeal the Test Act, and it were to be wished, That those who now-a-days endeavour, and write so much to have that Act annulled, would consider the late King William's Opinion of that Matter, whose Authority, and Memory they pretend so much to reverence and regard. He declared his just Aversion to repeal that Act, as being a thing that was contrary to all the Laws, and Customs of all Christian States, whether Protestants or Papists, who admitted none to a share in the Government, or publick Employments, but those who professed the publick and established Religion.* And those Men, who promoted the Occasional Bill, certainly paid a greater Respect to King William's Sentiments, than those who opposed it, and had that Bill been moved in his Reign, it had been agreeable to his Maxims of Government to have countenanced it.

I am very sensible, I have gone beyond the usual length of a Preface, and therefore must add no more, but desire my Reader not to think, I bear any ill will or enmity against those of the Presbyterian Perswasion in General, for I believe many of them are of most pious Conversations and honest Behaviours, and would be many more, were they not hurried on by the furious Passions and Zeal of their Ministers into many Violences and Extravagances; and therefore I have pretty strictly confined my self in this ensuing Piece, only to Examine into, and reflect on the unhappy conduct of their Ministers in the Times of the Rebellion, and its too sad a Truth to consider, how deep a share, those Men had in bringing on those Confusions, which makes it very surprizing, that any one in this Age should Write their Lives and applaud their Actions, which was the only way for others to lay open, and revive, their former rebellious Principles and Conduct; and I

---

* Fagel's Letter to Mr. Steuart wrote by the P. of Orange's direction.

can't but observe, how much the fatal Examples even of some of the Church of England Clergy have contributed to keep up the Life and Spirit of the Separatists, for when some of them have wrote most learned and unanswerable Treatises against the Dissenters, and have after many Years Observation and serious Consideration of Things, declared, they saw no reason to retract or alter any thing they had formerly Written ;* yet at the latter period of their Lives, by some fatal Influence, have acted and governed themselves by contrary Principles, which has given Occasion to the Dissenters to Triumph over those Books† they could never Answer, and to Boast, That when the Case was altered, the Authors were ashamed of them.

One Word to Mr. Palmer, and then I have done, which is to Defy him to except against the Authorities I've produced to make good my Assertions, I have not any where quoted the Scotch Presbyterian Eloquence, because I thought Arch. Spotsworth's History, and their own Printed Sermons, had as many Instances of the Blasphemy, Treason, and Nonsense of their Preachers ; and since he stands so much upon the Names of Authors being Prefixed to their Books,* I shall answer in the Words of one of their own Writers, viz. It is of no Importance who Writes, but what is Written.‡

---

* See Preface to the Friendly Debate.
† See Palmer against Westley.
‡ See Rights of the Proc. Dif. p. 70.

SEDITIOUS PREACHERS,

UNGODLY TEACHERS.

MY Chief Design in writing this Piece being to Demonstrate, That it was seditious Puritan Preachers who stirred up the People to the Rebellion in Forty one, and were the Cause of all those Confusions in Church and State; I think it will not be improper or foreign to my Purpose to look back and examine into the Loyalty of this Race of Men, when they first appeared in the World, whereby it will be evident, that an insolent Behaviour to Royal Authority, and an open Defiance to the Civil Magistrate were always inherent to their Principles, and that defaming of Governments with scurrilous Libels was their constant Practice, and that in despight of the Laws and the express Inhibition of the Crown, they held their Synods and their Classes, and formed their Presbyteries, and at length obliged that most Wise Princess Queen Elizabeth to punish them with Pillories and Gibbets for the Safety of her Crown and Person, and to enact Laws to suppress their outragious Insolencies, and she could never master their Confederacies and Clamours without extreme Justice; tho' at first she hoped to quiet them by her Lenity and Forbearance, but that only served to encourage and heighten their Boldness. So that it was not any pretended Ecclesiastical Severities in King Charles I. Reign, that

23

provoked them to rebell, and to desire the total Extirpation of
Episcopacy, but a furious Zeal to have their Darling Idol Presbytery
established as the Rule of Church Government and Discipline :
Which they had in vain tho' often attempted in the former Reigns.
And the Truth of these Assertions will most evidently appear from
the Testimony of that great Statesman Sir Thomas Walsingham, who
gives the following Account of the factious Zeal, which animated the
Puritans of his Time.

He first acquaints us with the Queens steddy Adherence to two
Maxims, the one was, not to force Consciences, the other was, not to
suffer factious Practices go unpunished, because they were covered
with the Pretences of Conscience ; and the Queen could never be
brought to deviate from these Rules, neither by the crafty Insinuations
of Courtiers, nor by the bold Clamours of restless Spirits, who laboured
to establish the Geneva Discipline, who as long as they only inveighed
against some Abuses, it was not their Zeal, but only their Violence
that was condemned, when they refused to comply with some Ceremonies, they were connived at with great Gentleness ; but it was observed that they affected Popularity much, and the Methods they
took to compass their Ends were judged dangerous. They set up
a new Model of Church Discipline, which was like to prove no less
dangerous to the Liberties of private Men, than to the Sovereign
Power of the Prince ; yet all this was born with as long as they
proceeded with those Expressions of Duty which became Subjects.
But afterwards when they resolved to carry on their Designs, without
waiting for the Consent of the Magistrate, and entred into Combinations, when they begun to defame the Government with ridiculous
Pasquils, and boasted of their Numbers and Strength, and in some
Places brake out into Tumults ; then it appeared, that it was Faction,
not Zeal, that animated them, and upon that the Queen found it
necessary to restrain them, yet she did it with all the Moderation,
that could consist with the Peace of the Church and State.*

---

* Compare this with Palmer's Vindication, page 90. Line 9.

We find this Account recited at large in the History of the Reformation, as the most authentic Relation of the Puritans Behaviour in that Queens Reign, by which the Author seems to justify the Necessity and Expediency of the Laws, which were then made to restrain and awe the Faction ; but how that Author came to change his Mind and declaim against those Laws as severe, and a Blemish to that glorious Reign, is not so easy to be reconciled ; especially when we consider, that he had formerly complained of that Queens Successors, for not holding the Reins of Government with the like Steadiness of hand which he thinks, would have prevented the Nation (how head-strong soever) from running into those desperate Confusions, which afterwards ensued.

In this Queens Reign this dangerous Position was first broached, viz. "That if Kings and Princes refused to reform Religion, the Inferiour Magistrates or People by direction of the Ministry, might lawfully, and ought if need required, even by Force and Arms to reform it themselves." A Doctrine very repugnant to the Queens Supremacy, and tending to raise disturbances in the State, whenever their unreasonable Demands are not complied with, and it was conformable to this Traiterous Assertion, that the Assembly of Divines met at Westminster, and published their Directory in Opposition to the express Commands of their Prince.

The Judicious Mr. Hooker acquaints us, how they affirmed that their Pastors, and Elders, ought to be in the Church, whether her Majesty and the State would or not, and how they threatned, that since neither their Suits to the Parliament, nor Supplications to the Convocation prevailed, we must blame our selves, if to bring in their Discipline, some such means should hereafter be used, as shall cause our Hearts to ake ; and accordingly we find them taking Advantage of the Necessities of the Government to be the most clamorous and insulting, and when the Danger of the Crown demanded their firmest Adherence and united Strength, then a separating Spirit divided them from the Unity of their Fellow Subjects.

The Dissenters now-a-days are very fond upon all occasions to

D   25

quote Father Fox the Martyrologist, and would fain have him be
thought to have favoured the Puritans ; but what Opinion the Good
Old Man entertained of them, he freely discovered in one of his
Letters, wherein he wonders what turbulent Spirit had possessed the
Factious Heads of the Puritans, and complains of their Bitterness
against him, for not Raving against the Church, as they did ; and for
his expressing himself with more Modesty and Concern for the
Publick Peace, than their furious Zeal would allow of. In short,
says he, they are a set of Men, who if they encrease and gather
strength, I am sorry to say, what disturbances my Mind Presages, they
will bring to the Nation, and how True a Prophet he has proved, let
every impartial Man judge.

Upon enquiry we may find, that no Order or Quality of Men
escaped their Insults, and that the Crown, the Parliament, the
Bishops and the Magistrates were too often the Subject of their con-
tumacious Impudence.

They protested to Her Majesty, that they would be no longer
Subject unto the Bishops unlawful and usurped Authority, and that
She maimed and deformed the Body of Christ, by maintaining the
established Government and rejecting theirs.

They tell the Parliament, for their not admitting the Platform set
down in their first Admonition, that it should be easier for Sodom and
Gomorrha in the Day of Judgment, than for such a Court ; and that
if they did not abrogate the Government by Bishops, they should be
in danger of the terrible Mass of God's Wrath, both in this Life and
in the Life to come.

They affirm, the Queen's Council may truly be said, to delight in
the Injury and violent Oppression of God's Saints and Ministers,
therefore the Lord would surely visit Them with an heavy Plague.

The Council cannot possibly deal truly in matters of Justice,
between Man and Man, because they bend all their Forces to bereave
Jesus Christ of his Government, and at this day they have taken
greater boldness, and grown more rebellious against the Lord, and his
Cause, than ever they were before.

But they reserved the choicest Flowers of their Rhetorick for the Bishops, and their Government.

They openly declared, that the Laws that maintained the Bishops are no more to be accounted of, than the Laws maintaining the Stews ; and then for the Bishops themselves they call them unnatural, false, and bastardy Governors of the Church, petty Antichrists, like incarnate Devils, that will lye like Dogs ; and that the worst Puritan was an honester Man, than the best Lord Bishop in Christendom ; and that truly great Prelate Archbishop Whitgift, a Man of great Wisdom and Moderation, who strove to bring them over to the Church with Gentleness and Forbearance, and who often interposed between them and the Gallows, Fines and Imprisonments, yet met with no suitable returns of Gratitude and Respect ; and now let impartial Posterity Judge, whether he deserved this dirty Ribaldry from them.

They said, of all the Bishops that ever were in the See of Canterbury, there was never any did so much hurt to the Church of God, as he hath done, that he was more Proud and Ambitious than Woolsey, more Tyrannical than Bonner, a very Antichristian Beast, the Belzebub of Canterbury. Even Bishop Jewel that great Light and Ornament of our Church, found it necessary to vindicate himself from the spightful Calumnies, of the Puritans, by a solemn Protestation made on his Death-bed. By this we may discover the Hypocrisy of Baxter and Calamy, who in a canting Style, tells us, that had the Bishops who succeeded Jewel been like him, they had been more honoured, and that Thousands who wished for good Bishops, were on the Parliaments side. Whereas Usher, Moreton, and even good Bishop Hall were deprived, sequestred, and plundered, with the same fury and malice, as the most obnoxious Bishops were : And how can these Men say, that the Puritans hoped and Waited to see tkeir way set up, when we are assured from undeniable Authorities, and from matters of Fact, that they Resolved to carry on their designs without waiting for the consent of the Magistrate, and that they did enter into Combinations, hold their Synods, and Form their Presbyteries, which

B. and C. would blind with the Name of Secret Conferences, but this
secret way of Conferencing has brought many a Man to the Gallows,
and within the Compass of the Law. If I should rake together all
the Rebellious Principles, Seditious Practices, and Billingsgate
Language of the Puritans in Q. Elizabeth's Reign, it were enough to
fill many Volumes ; whoever consults Whitgift and Bancroft's Writings, with Cambden's History, will wonder at the Superior Confidence
of those Men, who now-a-days can publickly avow, that the Puritans
always carried themselves with that Patience, Modesty, and Submission as became Christians, with the most exact Loyalty, and no manner
of Opposition.

When King James I. removed from Scotland, to take Possession of
the Imperial Crown of England, the Satisfaction he might reasonably
entertain of enjoying greater Honours, Power, and Authority, cou'd
not be more agreeable to his Mind, than his happy Deliverance from
the insupportable Tyranny of the Scottish Presbytery, and from the
Subjection to the ill manners, and insolent Practices of their Preachers,
whose furious Heat had drawn Tears from him in his tender Years,
and thought it their Honour to be always contending with him, whom
no Deserts could oblige, no Oaths or Promises bind, and that which
so much heighten'd their Boldness, was their resolute Adherence to
this safe Rule, That the King, nor his Council had any Authority to
judge of Treasons deliver'd in the Pulpit, but their Assemblies ought
to take Cognizance thereof ; and so whenever any of them was cited
before the Council, the rest made it a common Cause, and complained
that a wrong was done to the Kingdom of Christ, and would refuse to
censure them, nay so much as to remove a Preacher to another Congregation, that the King might not hear himself rail'd at to his Face,
or possibly some dire Woe denounced against him. To give a remark-
able Instance.

When the King found the Death of his Mother was intended, he
gave Orders to the Ministers to remember her in their publick
Prayers, which they refused to do, tho' the Prayer was most Christian,
and Lawful, and at the Request of their Sovereign, and on behalf of
28

their Sovereign, and on behalf of his Royal Mother. The King had appointed the Bishop of St. Andrews to pray before him upon that melancholy Occasion, the Ministers hearing of it, stirred up a young Man, not entred into the Function, to take the Pulpit, and exclude the Bishop, which the King finding at his Coming, call'd to him from his Seat, and told him, that Place was appointed for another; however, if he would remember his Mother in his Prayers, he might stay and proceed, which he refusing to do, the Guards pulled him down, whereupon he burst forth into bitter Expressions against the King, and then denounced a Judgment against the Inhabitants of Edinburgh.

Another Preacher, in his Pulpit, denounced the Curse against the King, that befel Jeroboam; that he should dye childless, and be the last of his Race. Upon which he was brought before the Council, where he confessed the Words, and proudly maintain'd them.

One of them, in his Pulpit, had called our Renowned Queen Elizabeth an Atheist, and a Woman of no Religion; upon the Complaint of the English Ambassador, he was cited before the Council, whereupon the Commissioners of the Church appeared in his Behalf, and declared, That if the Preacher should submit his Doctrine to the Tryal of the Council, then the Liberties of the Church, and the spiritual Government of the House of God would be quite subverted, and when some few diswaded them from his seditious Course, the greater Number cried out, It was the Cause of God, whereunto it concerned them to stand at all Hazards, and accordingly, the several Presbyteries subscribed a Form for the greater Confirmation of their Doings, and recommended the Cause in hand to God in their publick Prayers, and used their best Credit with their Flocks, for the Maintenance thereof. My Historian observes, that they would yield more to the Desires of the meanest People, than to the most reasonable Propositions of their King. Nay, so much were these Godly Ministers troubled with the Spirit of Opposition, That when the

King appointed a Thanksgiving, they would proclaim a Fast, and observe it too.

Now I will give my Reader an Instance or Two, how much these Ministers countenanced and incited the People to Rebellion, and were the only Trumpets to War. The King being surprized by some Lords, and closely confined, the Ministers were so far transported with Joy upon the King's Restraint, that they could not contain themselves within any Bounds, but went up the Streets of Edinburgh, after the manner of a Popish Procession, singing the 124 Psalm; and at their next General Assembly they ratifyed and approved of the King's Imprisonment, which was afterwards adjudged Treason by the three Estates of the Realm; at last the King found means to escape out of their Hands, but they would not allow him to be long at Ease, for the Ministers encouraged the People from their Pulpits to joyn with Bothwell, who was gathering Forces to invade the King, nor did their Folly and Madness stay there, but they gave those very Monies to the levying of Soldiers for Bothwell's Rebellion, which they had collected in their Churches for the Supply and Relief of the Protestants at Geneva then under great Troubles and Distresses.

These Proceedings of the Ministers obliged the King to offer certain Articles for their Subscriptions, *viz.* that all Preachers should yield Obedience; that they should not publickly revile his Majesty; that they should not draw the People from their due obedience to the King; that they should not alledge the Inspiration of the holy Spirit, when they should be accused of their seditious Sermons and Discourses; and yet the King could not obtain any Subscriptions from their Hands to these Points, which tended so much to secure the Honour of our holy Religion, the Welfare of the King, and the happy Settlement of the Kingdom.

I think it needless to insist upon the strict Correspondence, and the sweet Harmony, between the English and Scotch Disciplinarians, and how they afforded mutual Assistance, Refuge and Protection to each other, when ever they fled from the Hands of Justice, because our

Histories are so full and clear to those Matters; and besides I hasten to bring my Discourse nearer to my intended Design. No wonder, when King James came to England, that the Episcopal Clergy so readily obtained his Favour and Protection; here he found a learned moderate, and truly religious Ministry, there he had left a violent and factious one, who employed all their Study and Care, how they should best seduce and pervert the People from their Allegiance to him. And he very well knew, that the English Disciplinarians had often pressed their People with the Example of Scotland, and endeavoured to inveigle them into a good Opinion of their Proceedings and Platform, and had certainly brought the Nation into as great Confusions as ever Scotland was cursed with, had a Prince of tender Years wore the Diadem, or an easy Princes swayed the Scepter, but Queen Elizabeth's watchful Eye and strict Hand observed and broke all their Measures, and quashed all their Violence without any Noise or Tumult.

The King conceived that some of the Scottish Ministers might be moved by force of reason to quit their Opinions, and give Place to Truth, sent for several of them to Court to hear our Learned Bishops preach, where it grieved them to the Heart, says Spotsworth, to hear the Pope and Presbytery so often equalled in their Opposition to Sovereign Princes, The King endeavoured to gain these Men by easie and Gentle Methods, sometimes appointing publick, and often condescending to private Conferences with them, but it must be acknowledged an Error in his Government, that he loosen'd the Reins, which Queen Elizabeth had kept strict upon their Necks; for she was taught by Experience, that the Power of good Laws, and a steddy Administration of them, was the only effectual way to reclaim their turbulent Spirits; we dont find King James made any Examples of his Justice by some necessary Executions, as the Queen did, and yet the Dissenters in our days ungratefully reproach him, as laying the Foundation of all the Miseries they have since endured: but I believe, that if he had pelted them with sharper Weapons than Apothegms, he had subdued those unruly Tempters, which were at last so headstrong, as to overthrow both Church and State.

We are sensible enough of their Endeavours to blacken the Memory of that Prince, and why they wont look back and insist upon the Proceedings of Queen Elizabeth's Reign towards them, for then People would be rightly informed and understand, that both King James, King Charles and Archbishop' Laud used less severe means, and exercised fewer Acts of Power against them, than that the Queen had done before them, and so the implacable Hatred and the odious Reflections they are continually throwing upon those great Men, would be more obvious and exposed than they desire.

And those who are conversant in the History of those times must be sensible of the very great Disadvantages which Archbishop Laud in particular laboured under to recover the Honour and Purity of the Church, to restore it's former Orders, which had been so long neglected under the Jurisdiction of Abbot, who had been promoted to the See of Canterbury at the earnest Importunity of a Scotch Favourite ; and that Archbishop was as Ignorant of the true Constitution of the Church of England, of the State and Qualifications of the Clergy as his Scotch Patron ; to Abbots holding the See of Canterbury so many years, the Church in some Measure owed it's Downfal ; for it was he who filled it with so many Judas's, who betrayed it into the Hands of her Enemies, who persecuted those Hands which ordained them ; these were the Episcopal Men, whom Mr. Baxter and others have so often upbraided us with, who composed the Assembly at Westminster, and were accounted the Honour of the Parliaments Cause, but indeed the Disgrace and Reproach of their Mother Church, whom they had undutifully forsook in her greatest Extremity, and whose treacherous Apostacy made her the easier Prey to her more open Enemies.

We are told by the Noble Historian, that if Bishop Andrews or Overal had filled the See in Abbots room, they had quickly extinguished all that Fire in England, which had been kindled at Geneva, and that Infection would easily have been kept out, which could not afterwards be so easily expelled ; whereas Abbot made his House a Sanctuary to the most eminent of the factious Party, and licensed their most pernicious Books, and how much Envy, Malice, and ill Will must it needs bring to his Successor, when he laboured to retrieve the Antient Discipline of the Church, and to rescue her out of the Hands of weak and more false Men ; and it was the hard Fortune of that truly great and learned Prelate Archbiship Laud to succeed so unskilful a Pilot, who had run the Church upon Rocks and Shoals, and left her exposed open and defenceless to the Darts of her Enemies, and when he thought to bring her back into Haven, and to rescue her from his Predecessors Errors and Mistakes, to call them no worse, he soon found Peoples Tempers violent and impetuous, and their Insolence by former Indulgence, unbridled ; insomuch that the most necessary Reproofs and Censures were thought insupportable Injuries, and his honest Zeal in maintaining the Church, her Liturgy, Rites and Ceremonies in Decent Order and Oeconomy, was adjudged by a deluded Age a Design to intro-duce Popery, though his Learned Writings against the Jesuit ought to have set him beyond the least Suspicion. But his Enemies did not really think him a Friend to Rome, but an Enemy to Geneva, for the same day they adjudged him to dye, they voted out our Liturgy to make room for the Geneva Discipline.

It was King Charles the I. steddy Adherence to Episcopacy, and not giving way to their earnest Importunities for the abolishing of it, that was the Principal Cause of the great Rebellion against him, the first Tumults that were stirred up against him, proceeded from a religious Account, the Scotch raised Forces, provided Arms, and entred into solemn Leagues, and Bishop or no Bishop was the greatest Part of the Controversy ; for we must understand, that the King had set his heart upon a Uniformity of Worship thro' the whole Kingdom of Britain, and therefore had ordered a Lyturgy conformable to the English one for the Kingdom of Scotland, where King James his Father had got Episcopacy established by the Parliament, and the Assembly at Perth has made seueral other advances towards an Uni-

E   33

formity with England, and there seemed only to want the Liturgy
to compleat the Union ; but what Reception it met with, what
Tumults they raised to oppose it, I suppose, few Men are ignorant
of, nor of the more outragious Behaviour of their Kirk, which obliged
the king to dissolve them, however they continued to sit, and declared
Episcopacy unlawful, cited their Bishops before them, and pretended
Authority to Unbishop them.   They likewise voted down the Book
of Canons and the Articles of Perth, tho at that time established Laws
of their Kingdom, and which had been ratifyed by a former general
Assembly, they denied the King his Negative Vote, or Power to
meddle with Ecclesiastical Affairs, alledging, that the King took upon
him that Spiritual Power, which properly belonged to Christ as only
King and head of the Church, the Ministry and Execution whereof
was only given to such as bear the Ecclesiastical Government of the
same.   Now when we consider the Constitution of their General
Assemblies, we shall equally admire at the Folly and Iniquity of this
Doctrin.   There were about 260 Commissioners, and from every
Presbytery 3 or 4 Assessors, and from some Places 24 Lay Elders to
one Priest, all which Lay Elders have as great Power in Matters of
Doctrin and Discipline as the Priests themselves to judge and
pass definitive Sentences ; and the present Bishop of Sarum assures
us, That some of their Commissioners could neither write nor read,
and yet they were to judge of Heresy, and condemn Arminius his
Tenets.

However the Scotch Nation enter'd into Solemn Leagues and
Covenants to justify and defend the Proceedings of this Motly
Assembly, who threatned their Opposers with Excommunication, nay
with Damnation it self, and to give it the greater Authority, Cant an
eminent Presbyterian Preacher, assures the People in a Sermon
preached at Glasgow, that he was sent to them with a Commission
from Christ to bid them Subscribe the Covenant, which was Christs
Contract, and the Bishop of Sarum informs us, that the Ministers
inflamed the Nation into a War against their King by their Fasts and
Prayers, and their odd Application of the Scriptures.

Now its Foreign to my present Design to show by what dishonour-
able Management a Treacherous Peace was clapt up, insomuch that
all Men who had contributed to it, were ashamed of it, and its enough
to say that this Peace laid the Foundation of all our future Miseries,
all things being left with Circumstances very disgraceful to the King
to be settled by a Parliament, which was to be called in a short time
to meet at Westminster.

The prevailing Party in the House of Commons soon discovered a
great Disaffection to Episcopacy and the Church, partly in compliance
to the Scots, who quickly desired the House there might be an Uniformity of Religion between the Two Nations, for which Advice
they had the Thanks of the House, and to this end they received and
justified a Petition, from the Refuse of the People, that Episcopacy
might be abolished Root and Branch, and resolved upon the Question, that the Judicial Power of Bishops in the House of Peers ought
to be taken away, and accordingly ordered a Bill for that Purpose.
They troubled and punished those Divines, who had been most
Zealous for Conformity, and chose out Men of known and avow'd
disaffection to the Established Church to Preach before them.

By what I have already said, I easily conjecture that my Reader
will be before-hand with me in supposing that the Dissenters and
Puritan Conformist would not loose this hopeful opportunity, to set
up their darling Idol and pull down the Church, and by what vile
contrivances, and base methods, they did actually gain their Ends,
shall be my next business to show.

It has been already remark'd, that it was the Refuse of the People,
who Petitioned for the abolishing Episcopacy Root and Branch ; but
the Heads, Hearts, and Hands of their Clergy were the main Springs,
which moved and set it on Foot, and indeed the Petition medled
with very abstruse Points in Divinity, too sublime for Mechanick
Heads; not a Patent or Monopoly granted, nor the Price of any
Commodity raised, but these Men made Bishops the Cause.

" A Late Noble Historian informs us at large of their great disingenuity in procuring these Petitions, the Course was, first to prepare

a Petition very modest and dutiful, for the Form ; and for the Matter
not very unreasonable ; and then to communicate it at some Publick
Meeting, where care was taken it should be received with Approba-
tion : The Subscription of very few Hands filled the Paper itself,
where the Petition was written ; and therefore many more Sheets
were annexed, for the reception of the Number, which gave all the
Credit, and procured all the Countenance to the Undertaking ; when
a multitude of Hands was procured, the Petition itself was cut off ; a
new one framed, suitable to the Design in hand, and annexed to the
long List of Names, which were subscribed to the former : By this
means, many Men found their Hands subscribed to Petitions, of
which, they before had never heard of ; as several Ministers whose
Hands were to the Petition and Declaration of the London Ministers
before-mentioned have Professed to many Persons ; That they never
saw that Petition before it was presented to the House, but had
signed another, the Substance of which was, not to be compelled to
take the Oath enjoyned by the new Canons ; and when they found
instead of that, their Names set to a desire of an Alteration in the
Government of the Church, they with much trouble went to Mr.
Marshall, with whom they had intrusted the Petition and their
Hands ; who gave them no other Answer, but that it was thought
proper by those who understood Busines better than they, That the
latter Petition should rather be preferred than the former ; and when
he found, they intended by some publick Act to vindicate themselves
from that Calumny ; such Persons, upon whom they had their greatest
dependence, were engaged, by threats and promises to prevail with
them, to sit still, and to pass by that indirect Proceeding."

And Bishop Hall had an eye to this base Practice, when he tells
the Parliament, if that Underhand way of procured Subscriptions
could have reason to hope for favour in their Eyes ? But alas, they
so far prostituted the Honour of their House to these Wretches, that
when they Petitioned against Bishops Votes, they ordered their
Speaker to give them the Thanks of their House ; and the Royal
Martyr complains that at last they commanded and over-awed the

very Parliament ; for they usually came down in a most tumultuous
manner, that their confluence and clamour might prevail. "It
cannot be remembered without horror, that this strange Wild-fire
amongst the People was not so much, or so furiously, kindled by the
Breath of the Parliament as of their Clergy, who both administered
Fuel, and blowed the Coals in the Houses too ; These Men having
crept into, and at last driven out all Learned and Orthodox Men
from the Pulpits, had from the beginning of this Parliament, under
the Notion of Reformation, infus'd seditious Inclinations into the
Hearts of Men against the Government of the Church, with many
libellous Invectives against the State too, and as freely inveighed
against the Person of the King, as they had against the worst Malignant, profanely, and blasphemously applying whatsoever had been
spoken, and declared, by God himself, or the Prophets against the
most wicked and impious King, to incense and stir up the People
against their most Gracious Sovereign."

Thus they had recourse to their old way of libelling and reviling,
casting odious aspersions upon the Bishops, as void of Truth as of
good manners, by taxing them with favouring Papists and Popish
Doctrines, whereas those Prelates who felt the severest Marks of
their Rage and Malice, had spent their Time, their Strength, and
their Studies, in Preaching and Writing against Popery, and would
have Sacrificed all the Remains of their old Blood for the Maintenance of the Protestant Religion.

Then they insinuated, that the Bishops designed to introduce
Innovations into the Church, when those things the Prelates then
attempted to settle for the keeping up Decency and Order in the
Church, have been since thought necessary, and are now quietly
established into Custom, which shows how ill designing Men and
Leaders of Factions can improve things and affright People with
Shadows.

But above all they taught weak People, that the Prelates countenanced and avowed Arminius's Points, and discouraged the Preaching
up the Doctrines of Predestination, of Free Grace, Election for Faith

foreseen, and such like mysterious Theological Tenets, above the Thoughts and Conceptions of the most learned Part of Mankind; and it was strange, it should be made a matter of complaint to the Parliament, that the Clergy were faint-hearted, and fearful of Preaching their Congregations into Despair, by continually buzzing into their Ears, that God from all Eternity had reprobated and decreed them to Damnation, these things gave occasion to our famed Hudibras to Sing,

> That hard Words, Jealousies and Fears,
> Set Folks together by the Ears.

We cannot suppose the Bench of Bishops, which then abounded with so many learned and able Pens, were so far wanting to their own Innocence, as not to vindicate themselves from these senseless and false Calumnies, No! We find the very pious Bishop Hall attempting to put a stop to the Inundation of base and scurrilous Libels, and in an humble Remonstrance to the Parliament, he intreats them to check the daring and misgrounded Insolence of the Libellers, and complains that the Press had of late forgot to speak any Language, other than libellous; and therefore begs them to consider, what a shameful injustice it was in those bold Slanderers to cast upon the zealously religious Prelates, famous for their Works against Rome in foreign Parts, the Guilt of that, which they have so meritoriously and so convincingly opposed; and then in a Treatise at large, he asserted the Divine Right of Episcopacy, and offered his Reputation to Shame, and his Life to Justice, if any Man living could shew any one Lay Presbyter, that ever was in the Christian World, till Farell and Viret first created him, which was 1500 Years after the first Propagation of the Christian Religion.

One would have thought, that the superiour Worth, Learning, and Moderation of this aged Bishop would have Protected him from all rude Assaults, especially from those who would be thought Ministers of Christ, and Preachers of the Gospel; but no sooner had this great Prelate presented his humble Remonstrance to the Parliament, but Five of their new fangled Divines attack him under the Name of

Smectymnuus in such a scurrilous manner : That as Cambden observed
of the old Puritans, the Authors seemed rather Scullions out of the
Kitchin, than followers of Piety.

They could find no better Name for his Learned Arguments, than
calling them a heap of confident and groundless Assertions ; they tell
him, he sinned deeply against the Rules of Honesty, which in plainer,
but as true English, was calling him Rogue and Rascal. They likewise tell him, he acted with a Face of confident Boldness, and not
only forgot himself, but God also, and that he uttered Words border-
ing upon Blasphemy. But let us have done with this sort of Language,
fit only to drop from their Pens, whose Ink was as bitter as Gall, and
venemous as Poison. I shall only observe, that these Smectymnuuan
Zealots at that time overcome with the Tyranny of an ignorant
Zeal ; lived to see the Nation deliver'd from the Confusions they
had brought upon it, and then they desired to be thought Men of
the greatest Temper and Moderation, and not they, but some few
Sectarian Divines from New England were the only Incendiaries; but
for them weak Lambs, they were always for moderate Episcopacy,
and good Bishops : However, the Wisdom of the Nation thought it
necessary at the Restoration of the Church and State, to lay some
Restraints upon their Libellous Tongues, to secure their Establishment
and Perpetuity, and had they not cause enough to fence against
future Crimes ?

It may not be amiss to examine the particular Characters, that
Calamy gives to some of these Smectymnuan Zealots, by which it
will appear, that he only considered how to draw the Character of
an humble good Christian in general, and then clapt the Name of
one of his Confessors to it, without any Regard to the paaticular
Actions, Temper, or Writings of the Man : Thus Doctor Spurstow
(whom he takes care to let you know, was one of the Authors of
Smectymnuus) is distinguish'd by him for his meek, humble, and
peaceable Disposition ; now is not this very absurd ? First to own
him to be an Author of a most seditious and scandalous Libel, and
then call him a very humbly and peaceable Man. My Lord Clarendon

gives us a singular Instance of this Mans great Meekness and Humility, when he very fiercely told the King to his Face, That he would be damn'd, unless he consented to the utter abolishing of Episcopacy, and behaved himself with that Rudeness, as if he meant to be no longer subject to a King, no more than to a Bishop ; and our noble Author adds, that he lived after the Return of King Charles II. and according to the Modesty of that Race of People, came to kiss his Majesty's Hand, and continued the same Zeal in all seditious Attempts.

The next Character is that of Old Calamy, who tho' he was in his Judgment for the Presbyterian Discipline, yet he was of known Moderation towards those of other Sentiments, and that he was very Active to an Accommodation, and was one of those, who met in the Jerusalem Chamber with several Bishops, in which Meeting, by mutual Concessions, things were brought into a very hopeful Posture. Now he owns him to have been one of the Authors of the above-mentioned Libel, which certainly contradicts his pretended peaceable and accommodating Temper, for that Book was wrote on purpose to subvert the established Church, and as they themselves have boasted gave the first deadly Blow ; not to insist on the vile and unchristian Treatment, which the truly moderate Bishop Hall met with from their Hands, and then if we may give Credit to old Calamy's own Testimony, we have it from his own Mouth, that he was the chief Instrument in framing and encouraging the Root and Branch Petition, for he boasts that it was formed in his House before the Beginning of the long Parliament. Now mark the Villany and Hypocrisy of this Man, he meets the Bishops in the Jerusalem Chamber, in order to accommodate Matters, and pretends to them to be of an healing Temper ; when at the same time, he had a Petition in his Pocket to desire the Parliament totally to abolish the established Government of the Church, which was delivered, and had their wished for Success. With the same Air of Truth we are told, that this Man kept his Temper and Moderation after his Ejectment, whereas he was the very first Man, who committed any open Violation to the Act of Uniformity, and suffered for it accordingly.

Thus from these Two contradictory and absurd Characters, we may make a Judgment of the Rest, and know how to credit little Calamy's Relations both of Men and Things.

It was the Votes and Resolutions of the House of Commons, which animated the seditious Party, and added Life and Vigour to their outragious Insolencies ; for at the Beginning of the Parliament, the Puritan Faction published a Sham Order in the Name of the House of Commons assembled in Parliament, to stir up and invite Active Men to accuse Ministers, which Order (tho disclaimed within the Walls of the House, yet they had not Virtue enough to countermand it, nor to enquire into the Publishers of it,) occasioned many Petitions against the Clergy ; for if any Knave or Fool bore any ill Will to his Minister, or did not care to pay his Tyth, he presently got Two or Three base Mechanicks to sign a Petition, which constantly run in the Name of the whole Parish, tho Three Parts in Four had never seen it, but disowned it under their Hands, then it was no hard matter to procure false Witnesses ; for said they, the Parliament put no man to his Oath, nor give any Costs or Damages upon Default of Proof ; and so many a Clergyman, after a chargeable and vexatious Attendance, and sometimes Imprisonment, has been dismissed from their Committees, without so much as reproving the false Witness, or censuring the malicious Accuser.

And it often happened, that a Minister was called upon to answer for some Doctrinal Points he had preached perhaps Twenty Years before, as many were for saying, That Baptism washeth away Original Sin, and one was for saying, That the Blessed Virgin was the Mother of God ; then must he give a Fee to a common Lawyer to plead for him at the Bar of the House, and prove the Soundness of his Doctrine.

A Complaint was made to the House, that Doctor Couzens endeavored to seduce a young Student to embrace Popery, and that his Friends were obliged to remove him from the College to prevent it ; whereas the Doctor made it appear by several Members of their own House, that he being Vicechancellor of Cambridge, upon Examination,

F

found the Party Mr. Nichols guilty of holding Popish Tenets, whereupon he made him publickly recant his Popery, and then expelled
him the University.

In some Cases they betrayed their great Malice, and notorious
Ignorance, Doctor Stern was charged with Blasphemy, for only
writing round the Bason for gathering Alms, Honour God with thy
Substance.

Indeed, Mr. White the Chairman of the Committee published a
List of scandalous and malignant Priests, which he called his first
Century, being the Names of one hundred Divines sequestred for
scandalous Enormities ; and the Enemies of our Church at this day
reproach us with this black List, and appeal to it to justify the Parliaments Proceedings, to throw all possible Scandal on the Clergy of
that time ; but whoever slightly looks over that List, will soon
discover great Malice and Disingenuity in the Publisher, for of the
Hundred Instances he produces, Malignancy against the Parliament,
or a Neglect of some of their Orders is an objected Crime against
more than Fourscore of them, and yet the only Design of the Publisher was, (as appears by his Preface,) to represent the Body of the
Clergy as Men of vitious Lives and scandalous Conversations, and
that the Prelates who ordained them into the Ministry were justly
deprived, and their Government in the Church with great Reason
abolished. But in Truth, Conformity to the Church, and Loyalty
to the King, made these Ministers so obnoxious to their Faction,
who had waged War against the King, and appointed Monthly Fasts
to be observed for the Success of their Arms, and it's a main Article
against many in this List, that they did not religiously observe these
Fasts in their Churches ; and then they requir'd them to take the
Covenant to capacitate them to hold their Livings, where they swear
with all Sincerity, Reality, and Constancy, to defend and preserve
the King's Majesties Person ; now to keep this Oath, and yet to fast
and pray for the Success of those Men, who were then firing in the
Face of the King, was such a Contradiction, as the evading Pens of
a Baxter or Calamy can't reconcile : These were those Blessed times,

when swearing was a Sin, but forswearing a Duty; for when Mr. White required Dr. Featly to take the Covenant, he refused, and alledged that it was contrary to his Oath of Allegiance to his Sovereign, and contrary to his Oath of Canonical Obedience to his Bishop; whereupon White told him, he must suffer and be turned out, to which the good Man replied, "Nec mihi ignominiosum est pati, quod pasus est Christus, nec tibi gloriosum est facere, quod fecit Judas." And its no Wonder, that White dyed distracted in the midst of his Rage against the Church, crying out, how many Clergymen, their Wives and Children he had ruined.

Reader, think it not strange, that I undertake to demonstrate from this truly scandalous List, that the Clergy of this time was generally Men of Vertue and unexceptionable Lives and Conversations; Mr. W. in his Preface tells his Reader, he should have an Essay of the Gall and Wormwood of the Episcopal Government taken out of London the Metropolis, and by that he should see, what Vermin crawled upon and devoured the principal and vital Parts.

Now there are 123 Parishes within the Bills of Mortality, and yet we find but 7 Names recorded in this formidable List, who belonged to those Parishes, and of that very small number, some were not taxed with the least Immorality; one was for only writing a Book, to prove it Sacrilege to take away the Lands of Deans and Chapters, and that the Parliament perverted the Will of the Dead that gave them. Others was, for expressing great Malignancy against the Parliament, which indeed was the Burthen of the Song through the whole List. Now if the London Clergy, who were immediately under the watchful Eye of the Parliament, had so trifling a Number liable to their severest Scrutiny; I think we may safely conclude, that the Prelates of that time had taken great Care to fill the Churches of London with Men of great Piety and unexceptionable Lives. Besides Bishop Juxon and his immediate Predecessor Laud were acknowleg'd by their greatest Enemies to have been Men of Eminent Piety and strict Manners, who sure would never have suffered a debauched and careless Clergy to have disgraced their Diocese.

I shall farther observe, that there was 115 Ministers sequestred and turned out of the 123 Parishes above mentioned, which shews how little regard ought to be had to what Baxter, or his Abridger, relate for certain Truths, for they both averr, that those who were sequestred were proved insufficient and scandalous ; and that those who were cast out for the War alone, as for Opinion sake, were comparatively few.

But it may be objected in Answer to this, that Mr. Baxter has elsewhere affirmed the contrary, and at a time too when he may be reasonably supposed to have spoken his Thoughts more freely ; for he tells us in his holy Common-wealth, that the Parliament displaced many in the Universities upon the Account of Religion, and that they cast out abundance of Ministers upon the same Account. Whoever is the least conversant in Mr Baxter's Life and Conversation, knows that Richard and Baxter were continually mortifying one another. However the Slips of a Treacherous Memory are far more excusable, than the bold Assertions of notorious Falsities, for Mr Baxter more than once affirms that White published two Centuries of scandalous Ministers, which is a Falsity as black and malicious as the Assertions and Scandals he intended thereby to throw upon the Church and her Ministers.

A noted Author, who lived and wrote in the Heat of the Rebellion, mentions Whites first Century, but avows, that to his Knowledge there never came forth a Second, and that when some solicited his Majesty for Leave to set forth a Book of the vicious Lives of some Parliament Ministers, his Majesty blasted the Design, least the Common Enemy the Papist might take the Advantage of it. And I never could find upon the strictest Enquiry, that any one ever saw this second Century. But Mr. Calamy tho' an Abridger, is yet more particular in this matter than Mr. Baxter, no doubt it was to show his Readiness to publish any Slanders that might blacken the Episcopal Clergy ; for he tells the World, that White, or the Chairman of the Committee was the Publisher of a Century of scandalous Ministers, which was afterwards followed with a second Century, both filled with most abominable Particularities : I wish Mr. Calamy may have the Grace before he comes to dye, to repent of the publishing such false Scandal, malitiously designed to blacken and vilify the most Grave, Holy, and learned Clergy at that time in the whole Christian World.

From all these things it appears, by what laudable Methods, they got Episcopacy extirpated, and the Ministers ejected, viz. By stirring up the Refuse of the People to deliver their Petitions in the most tumultuous Manner, and then by downright Forgery in procuring Hands to those Petitions, which never wanted false Witnesses and malicious Accusers to abett and support them ; and lastly, by scandalous Libells and Invectives, Methods so directly Irreligious, that it plainly appeared, their Dispute was no longer Matter of Scruple and Worship, but Superiority and Power.

And this New Race of Saints having seized by Fraud, and Violence, the Office and Livings of all Orthodox and Learned Men, soon spirited up the People into a Rebellion, and involved them in Blood and Confusion ; for had they permitted the Nation to enjoy it's former Peace and Tranquility, then the Poor sequestred Clergy might have appealed to the known Laws of the Realm and impartial Justice must have restored them to their just Rights ; or had the King remained in Possession of his Legal Power and Authority, he never would have suffered those outragious Proceedings against the Clergy, so that it unhappily became the Interest of the factious Ministers to affright the People with the Danger of their Religion, and the Necessity of a farther Reformation, and then engaged them in a Religious War, to accomplish their Ends, and secure to themselves a full Possession of other Mens Properties.

There might be produced innumerable Testimonies, from several Historians, to prove the Guilt and Activeness of the Puritan Ministers in sounding the Trumpet to War, but the single Authority of my Lord Clarendon will be sufficient to our Purpose ; who in many Places of his incomparable History complains of the great Licence, which was exercised in preaching, and the Judges not assuming

Courage to question their preaching such scurrilous seditious, Discourses, made those Plants grow up and prosper to a full Harvest of
Rebellion and Treason ; and whoever consults that noble History,
will find very extraordinary instances of their Perjury, Rebellion, and
unheard of Insolencies to the Person of their distressed King, and
how they administered Fuel, and blew up the Coals in the Houses
too, and by their Infectious Breaths furiously kindled the strange
Wildfire that animated the People to so many Insolencies ; there
are, says our great Historian, Monuments enough in the seditious
Sermons at that time printed, and in the Memory of Men, of others'
not Printed, of such wresting and perverting of Scripture to the
odious Purposes of the Preacher, that pious men will not look over
without trembling, and then goes on and names several Texts with
the wicked Applications that were made to them. It would fill a
Volume, says he, to insert all the impious Madness of this kind,
and leaves them with this lasting Mark of Infamy : No good Christian can without Horrour think of those Ministers of the Church,
who by their Function, being Messengers of Peace were the only
Trumpets to War, and Incendiaries towards Rebellion. How much
more Christian was that Athenian Nun, in Plutarch, and how shall
She rise up in Judgement against those Men, who, when Alcibiades
was condemned by the publick Justice of the State, and a Decree
made, that all the religious Priests and Women should Ban and Curse
him, stoutly refused to perform that Office, answering that she was
professed Religious, to Pray and to Bless, not to Curse and to Ban,
and then goes on and says, that if the Person and the Place can
improve and aggravate the Offence (as without doubt it doth both
before God and Man) methinks the preaching Treason, and Rebellion,
out of the Pulpit, should be worse than the advancing of it in the
Market, as much as Poisoning a Man at the Communion should be
worse than murthering him at a Tavern.

Had not the Royal Martyr too much reason so often to complain
to his Parliament of the bold Licence in preaching Sermons so full
of Bitterness, and Malice, against the Laws established, so full of
46

Sedition against his own Person and the Peace of the Kingdom, that
he was many times amazed to consider by what Eyes those things
were seen, and by what Ears they were heard.

The Dissenters now-a-days would have us believe, that the War
begun upon a Civil Account, but sure those that lived in that time
knew best upon what Grounds they took up Arms, and incited others
to do the like, and that it was for the Cause of Religion, and Reformation, will most evidently appear from the following Considerations.

When the Parliament was to borrow Mony of the City to carry on
the War, they employed the Ministers to Harangue the Citizens
assembled at Guild-hall, with the seasonableness and necessity of
their being liberal in their Contributions, in order to preserve their
Religion then in imminent danger.   It was upon one of these Grand
Solemnities, "that old Calumy a loud Trumpeter to War, gave his
Mighty and Omnipotent Arguments to perswade them to a Liberal
Contribution, but at the same time raised this very Pertinent Objec-
tion, Why should the Ministers engage themselves so much in this
Business?   Why, says he, to procure a Religious Peace, that may
continue the Gospel amongst us, and bring a Reformation, such as
all the Godly in the Kingdom desired ; he tells them they might
easily have a French Peace, that would bring a Massacre with it ;
(which was a bold Intimation that the King designed it) and then
goes on to justify his own conduct, by informing them, that the
Priests in the Old Testament sounded the Silver Trumpets to War ;
and if this was the way of God, certainly much more in such a Cause
as this, where Religion is so intwined, and indeed so interlaced, that
Religion and This Cause like Hippocrates his Twins, they must live
and dye together.   And Gentlemen, says he, if Religion were not
concern'd in this Cause, and Mightily concerned to, and if Religion
did not live and dye with it, We had not appeared this day ; and
then least they should be faint-hearted, and pretend they were
exhausted with their continual Demands, our Divine tells them, that
Jesus Christ emptied himself of his Divinity to make us rich, and shed
his Blood for them ; you have not yet made your selves so Poor as

Jesus Christ was, that had no House to lodge in, and he did all this for
your sakes; you have not yet shed your Blood for the Cause of Christ :
We read that Moses was willing to be blotted out of the Book of
Life for the Cause of God, and will you not venture your earthly
Provisions for so Good a Cause as this. Religion hath produced all
your Wealth you have, all your Wealth is but the Child of Religion,
(tho' it was ten to one but many of his Auditors got their Wealth by
Sequestring, and Oppressing, the Kings most faithful Subjects) and
then I hope your Riches will preserve Religion ; and let me assure
you on the Word of a Minister, the contributing to this Cause for
God's sake ; for the Glory of God, and for the Peace of the Gospel,
will be a means to make you the sooner ascend up Jacob's Ladder,
not for the giving the Mony, but for the Evidence of your Faith,
through the Merits of the Lord Jesus Christ, by your giving of the
Mony ; happy Mony, that will purchase the Gospel, Religion, and
Reformation to our Posterity, and I count it the greatest Opportunity,
that ever God did offer to the godly of this Kingdom, to give them
some Money to lend to this Cause, the Lord give you Hearts to
believe this (and we find great was their Faith, for the City at that
time contributed a very large Summ to carry on the War) and here is an
Extraordinary Appearance of so many Ministers to encourage in this
Cause, that you may see how real the godly Ministry in England is
unto this Cause, and I speak in the Name of these Reverend Ministers, that we will not only speak to perswade you to contribute,
but every one of us have already lent and will lend to our utmost
Power."

Ingram Content Group UK Ltd.
Milton Keynes UK
UKHW020643140423
420171UK00006B/217

9 781376 614350